The Essence of Human Nature

About the Author and Respondent

MARK P. COSGROVE

Mark Cosgrove is an assistant professor of psychology at Taylor University, in Upland, Indiana. He obtained his B.A. at Creighton University and his M.S. and Ph.D. in experimental psychology from Purdue University. He was a research associate and visiting assistant professor in the Department of Psychology at Purdue in the fall of 1973 before serving as a research associate with Probe Ministries International from 1974 to 1976. He is a member of Sigma Xi—the Scientific Research Society of North America, Midwestern Psychological Association, and the American Scientific Affiliation. Dr. Cosgrove has published frequently in *Vision Research* and in *Perception and Psychophysics*. He has been a guest lecturer in the classrooms of such universities as the University of Calgary, Colorado State University, Michigan State University, and Cal State Fresno.

MARTY J. SCHMIDT

Marty J. Schmidt is assistant professor of psychology at the University of New Hampshire. His formal education was at Purdue University, where he received his B.S., M.S., and Ph.D. degrees, the latter in experimental psychology. He is the author of two books, *Understanding and Using Statistics: Basic Concepts* and *Vision and Audition: The Psychology and Physiology of Seeing and Hearing*.

His research papers have been printed in *Perception & Psychophysics, Vision Research, Psychonomic Science,* and the *Journal of Experimental Psychology: Human Perception and Performance*. Dr. Schmidt serves as an article referee for the *Journal of the Experimental Analysis of Behavior* and as editorial consultant for various publishing companies. He is a member of the Eastern Psychological Association, the Midwestern Psychological Association, the Association for Research in Vision and Opthalmology, the Optical Society of America, and Sigma Xi.

The Essence of Human Nature

Mark P. Cosgrove

with a response by
Marty J. Schmidt

ZONDERVAN PUBLISHING HOUSE
OF THE ZONDERVAN CORPORATION
GRAND RAPIDS, MICHIGAN 49506

PROBE MINISTRIES
INTERNATIONAL
RICHARDSON, TEXAS 75080

Copyright © 1977 by Probe Ministries International

Printing History Third printing   December 1977

Library of Congress Cataloging in Publication Data

Cosgrove, Mark P
   The essence of human nature.

   (Christian free university curriculum)
   Bibliography: p.
   1. Psychology—Philosophy.   2. Man.
   3. Christianity—Psychology.   I. Title.
   II. Series.
   BF38.C75   150'.1   77-9612

ISBN 0-310-35711-X

Place of Printing *Printed in the United States of America*

Permissions

page 43 Reprinted from *Physical Control of the Mind* by José M.R. Delgado. Vol. 41 of *World Perspectives,* planned and edited by Ruth Nanda Anshen. New York: Harper & Row, 1969.

page 45 Courtesy of Dr. Neal E. Miller

page 55 Reprinted from *Psychology Today,* January, 1974. Copyright © 1973 by Ziff-Davis Publishing Company. All rights reserved.

page 59 Courtesy of NASA

Design Cover design by Paul Lewis
Book design by Louise Bauer

What is Probe?

Probe Ministries is a nonprofit corporation organized to provide perspective on the integration of the academic disciplines and historic Christianity. The members and associates of the Probe team are actively engaged in research as well as lecturing and interacting in thousands of university classrooms throughout the United States and Canada on topics and issues vital to the university student.

Christian Free University books should be ordered from Zondervan Publishing House (in the United Kingdom from The Paternoster Press), but further information about Probe's materials and ministries may be obtained by writing to Probe Ministries International, Box 5012, Richardson, Texas 75080.

Book Abstract

Current evidence is examined from psychological research which points to the inadequacy of those views of human nature which describe man as just material, totally determined, and as only a higher animal. A critical evaluation is made of recent brain control experiments, the deterministic model of B. F. Skinner, and language studies in chimpanzees.

Contents

Illustrations

chapter one

The Pressing Question

Chapter Abstract

The mystery of human nature has been debated through the centuries. Some theories have been helpful to man, others harmful. The difficult study of man still seems far from resolved.

The Pressing Question

Harry Benson was a successful computer scientist — until he became a human time bomb! The story began with an automobile accident that resulted in brain damage. Months after the accident, Harry suffered from occasional blackouts, during which he went berserk and brutally assaulted innocent bystanders. Then a famous medical research team planted forty tiny electrodes in Harry's brain and connected him to a miniature computer. But something went wrong. Through a terrifying miscalculation, Harry was overwhelmed by the urge to kill for three minutes each day! This is an unbelievable portrayal of the lead character in Michael Crichton's novel *The Terminal Man.*[1] Warner Brothers turned this novel into a suspense-thriller movie.

Though only fictional, Harry Benson represents a current scientific view of man. Man is a biological machine — complicated and intelligent — but machinery nonetheless. Such a view is not without its 11 consequences. It is especially important to clarify our understanding of the nature of man because our view of human nature affects critical issues of society, such as capital punishment, abortion, and biological and psychological engineering, to name a few. In addition, every school of thought on the nature of man promotes a corresponding theory or method of counseling to solve our problems. For example, biological views of man and his problems give rise to such medical approaches to therapy as the use of electrode implants and prefrontal lobotomy (cutting the nerves to the frontal lobes of the brain). Behavioristic views of man give rise to behavior-modification therapy. Humanistic views have given us transactional analysis and myriads of group therapies. The accuracy of each particular view of man suddenly becomes important because we must decide who can best treat our anxiety, our marriage difficulties, and other disconcerting experiences.

One of the disciplines in which man is studied today is psychology, the science of human and animal behavior. Psychology is currently one of the most popular subjects on the college campus and its data and theories concerning man have a powerful impact not only in the academic world but in the popular press and television as well. Psychology is an excellent discipline from which to view man, because it considers a broad range of past theories and practices as well as the latest scientific methods of analysis and treatment. Also, it is extensive enough as a field to gather data from many subdisciplines, from physiological psychology to social psychology. Its breadth of study and method has thus produced several major schools of thought, including behavioristic, psychoanalytic, humanistic, and transpersonal models. These schools have debated among themselves many of the key issues about man. Such intramural debates can stimulate good research.

The investigation into the mystery of human nature is certainly as old as man himself. While early man's thoughts about himself are not readily available to us, we can see that from the pre-Socratic Greek philosophers to the modern neurophysiologists, men have

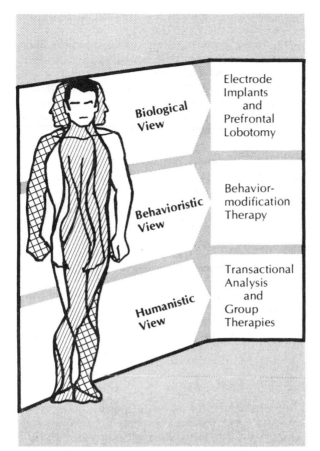

Biological
View

Electrode
Implants
and
Prefrontal
Lobotomy

Behavioristic
View

Behavior-
modification
Therapy

Humanistic
View

Transactional
Analysis
and
Group
Therapies

Different views of man result in different attempts to solve man's problems.

vigorously debated the issues surrounding human nature. What is the relationship of man's nature to material and immaterial reality? Does man act out of free
will, or is his behavior determined? Is he good or evil
in his inner being? What should be the basis of his
morals? What are the sources of his mental ills and his
lack of fulfillment? Anthropology, biology, history,
literature, philosophy, psychology, sociology, and
theology have contributed their answers to these questions and represent forums in which man has been
considered. A list of the commentators on the subject
reads like *Who's Who* in the Scholar's Hall of Fame:

philosopher greats like Plato and Aristotle, Descartes and Kant; church scholars like Augustine and Aquinas; scientists like Weber, Fechner, Helmholtz, Wundt, and Pavlov; and modern psychological theorists like Freud, Watson, Skinner, and Maslow.

Surprisingly, the accumulated wealth of knowledge from the past several thousand years has advanced us only slightly in our understanding of human nature. Even with the aid of scientific technology in fields like psychology and biology, the critical study of man has lagged far behind the success of the physical sciences in their exploration of the nature of matter. Dr. J. A. Wheeler, professor of physics at Princeton, indicated in an article for *American Scientist* that scientists still hope for a breakthrough in the difficult study of man. He said:

> Today no mystery more attracts the minds of distinguished pioneers from the field of molecular biology than the mechanism of brain action. Participating in the exploration are workers from fields as far removed from one another as neurophysiology, anatomy, chemistry, circuit theory and mathematical logic. Many feel that the decisive step forward is waiting for an idea, an as-yet-undiscovered concept, a central theme and thesis. Whatever it will prove to be, we can believe that it will somehow touch the tie between mind and matter, between observer and observed.[2]

Unfortunately, no breakthrough in the understanding of man's nature seems near. Part of the problem, of course, is the difficulty of the subject matter. Man's brain is highly complex, and his research tool is at the same time the subject under investigation. Did Sherlock Holmes ever confront such a challenge? Some scientists feel that this problem alone — having to explain man by man — means that we can never completely understand ourselves. This limitation, however, should not deter us from pursuing a knowledge of the nature of man. Gaining knowledge, even though it be partial, is at least progress, in any field.

The Presuppositions and Methods of Psychology

Chapter Abstract

Modern psychology's historical roots are examined, circa 1850, when empiricism and the new theory of evolution were emphasized. These roots are shown to affect even present experimental psychology, which still neglects the immaterial part of man that gives human life its uniqueness, meaning, and purpose.

The Presuppositions and Methods of Psychology

Before looking at the data of psychology on human nature, one must first look at the climate in which psychological data are gathered — the "filters" through which the experimental data are sifted and interpreted. The psychologist, like other scientists, has certain prior beliefs or presuppositions about his subject matter, the nature of scientific inquiry, and the immediate data to be collected. These presuppositions have a major effect on how he designs experiments and how he decides to treat the findings, especially those negative to his hypothesis. Presuppositions that represent a "working view" or model of the world are necessary to science. However, when they become inflexible, rigid, absolute "truths," they cripple the honest pursuit of knowledge.

To discover the presuppositions of modern psychology in its study of the nature of man, we must trace its historical roots back to the time before the founding of the first psychological laboratory in 1879 by Wilhelm

Wundt. No era is without its speculations about man's nature, and the mid-1800s is a pointed example. The events and ideas immediately preceding 1879 have had a profound role in shaping the presuppositions of psychology.

Empiricism

The first "root" of modern psychology is a way of thinking called *empiricism*. In the early 1800s, this approach to knowledge snuffed the desire of scientists to study the "soul" or immaterial mind of man. Empiricism taught that one could know only that which was discernible by the physical senses. In fact, some empiricists believed that if any concept was not accessible to the senses it did not exist. In theory, this was a denial of the existence of all nonphysical reality, and reality began to be redefined by only what physical senses or instruments could measure. And so the seeds of thought were planted that later grew into the idea that any nonphysical part of man, if it existed at all, was not open to investigation. With the body and the mind separated by this dualistic thinking and the body so easily accessible to measurement, the natural tendency was for the later psychologist to ignore the mind or soul in their pursuit of the nature of man. It is clear that empirical methods cannot measure that which is not material; but to conclude from this that the immaterial part of man does not exist is unwarranted, being based strictly on subjective presuppositions and not on science.

Evolution

The second historical "root" that affected the presuppositions of psychology — and hence its methods and theories — was the *theory of evolution*. Darwin's *Origin of Species*[3] was published in 1859, and the popularization of the theory of man's evolution from lower primates began to restrict explanations of man's nature to those attributes and processes that could result from a biological, evolutionary system. If empiricism made man just physical, then evolution helped to make him just animal.

It is important to remember that these general beliefs

on the essence of human nature were accepted before any serious collection of data began in the laboratories of psychology. It was inevitable, then, that these beliefs (i.e., that everything about man can be explained by that which is physical and by that which is animal) would influence the new field of psychology from its very beginnings. In 1860, Gustav Fechner published his *Elements of Psychophysics* (English translation title). In the preface he asserted that he was going to specify the relationship between physical events (stimuli) and mental events (sensation strength) with a mathematical equation.[4] By the time Wundt established his laboratory in 1879, philosophic, not scientific, presuppositions had already determined what form the study of man would take. Following the lead of Fechner's title, this first laboratory was called a laboratory of "psychophysics." The *psyche,* from the Greek word for "soul," or essential nature of man, was to be explained by *physics,* or "matter"; hence the reason for the joint name — psychophysics.

Consistent with these presuppositions, then, the mainstream of experimental psychology has chosen to study the behavior of man and animals. After all, it is the behavior of the body that one can observe with the senses and quantify in some empirical fashion. In psychology this involves the use of operational definitions. For example, three dates with the same person or a certain degree of sexual arousal could be used as an operational definition of human love, since such examples of behavior are observable and countable. The use of operational definitions allows experimenters to manipulate the variable of human love in some sort of controlled fashion. However, there is a marked tendency to disregard intangible human qualities simply because they cannot be observed or quantified in this scientific way. Such tendencies follow the empiricist's presupposition that all there is to man is what we can scientifically observe.

By scientific observation, of course, we mean the accurate measuring of material events such as behavior. This pressing question remains, however: Have we accurately defined love when we have described and quantified dating behavior or sexual re-

sponse? Can one write, "Love equals three dates,"
and in so doing correctly define love? Or can we say,
"A man equals a set of numbers describing his activities and physiological states," and thereby correctly describe a human being?

Because of the evolutionary presuppositions of
psychology, psychologists have also felt a great deal of
freedom to study animal subjects and generalize to
human nature. Animal research is justified on its own
merits, and it is a useful method to discover things
about man when experimentation on human subjects is
unethical or impossible. There are key research areas,
such as brain research, where the study of animals has
provided nearly all the evidence for the models and
theories on human nature. It is assumed that the simi-
larity of man to other primates is great enough to
warrant explaining man in terms of animal motivation
and behavior.

Thus, the presuppositions of psychology and the
resulting methods have produced a proliferation of
models of human nature, such as physiological and
behavioral models, that use data to give a very materialistic and animalistic view of man. Empiricism denies that the immaterial exists; therefore, man is only
matter. If only the material exists, then *every* effect of
man's life has a material and fatalistic cause. Therefore, man is mechanical and determined. Men and
animals share the same material; therefore, men are
only animals. What is being lost or disregarded
through this process are all those models or views of
man that argue for his immaterial essence: his self-
consciousness, his free choice, his rational thought,
his unique culture, and much more.

There are those who resist this as an oversimplifica-
tion, pointing out that the materialistic, behavioristic
views of man's nature have had adverse effects on
man. With the loss of his humanity, man becomes
hollow, the victim of impersonal environmental
forces. If he is to live his life in the light of what he
believes about his own meaning and purpose, then his
values, loves, dreams, responsibilities, self-concept,
and most important, his purpose, all become lost. He is
destined to live life with his feelings telling him one

thing about himself, and "science" insisting on something quite different.

The study that follows will set aside the materialistic, behavioristic presuppositions about man and investigate his nature by analyzing the best psychological data available. Our investigation will lead us to examine three questions: first, Is man just material? second, Is man's behavior determined? third, Is man just an animal? The data within psychology and brain physiology will show that man cannot be completely described by the material (though he is undoubtedly material) or completely by the mechanical (though much of his behavior is described by laws of cause and effect) or completely by animal nature (though he is undoubtedly a conscious creature with a body), but that he is uniquely more. He is truly man.

Is Man Just
Material?

Chapter Abstract

Experiments showing that the immaterial mind seems to be a separate function and entity from the material brain are considered. If these are correct, then scientific presuppositions that the physical world is a closed system must be revised.

Is Man Just Material?

There is first the need, then, to examine the evidence for the ''mind,'' or the immaterial self of man — the part of him that is self-conscious as well as thinking and feeling. The issue at stake is this: Does any mental function exceed the activity of the brain? Are all mental functions and brain activities one and the same? A simple materialistic explanation for all that man is and does will not fit with human experience or with what is known about the human brain.

Men throughout history have believed in the existence of the mind and not for shallow reasons. First of all, one intuitively knows that the mind exists, i.e., by being aware of it as it is perceiving, imagining, thinking, resolving, hoping, fearing, and loving. Matter can be known by sense perception, but mind is known by self-consciousness. One can see color and taste food, but how are intangibles like fears or thoughts apprehended? It is obvious from this that mind and matter must have at least some different properties.

25

Scientists can measure and record a brain state when a person is in pain, but they can never record what it feels like for him to be in that state. One does not experience the occurrence of a nerve firing; he does experience the feeling of pain, or anger, or love, etc. Granted, the brain is integrally and necessarily involved in this experience (as a blow on the head would demonstrate), but is this sufficient reason to *equate* human experience in its entirety with brain activity?

Now some would argue against an immaterial mind on the grounds that matter (brain) and nonmatter (mind) could never interact, since nonmatter has no capacity to cause — is incapable of producing an effect — in the material realm. Therefore, how could one assert that a mind state (i.e., a desire to raise an arm) could cause a brain state that would give the appropriate nerve impulses for arm movement? How-

Are man's actions simply a result of brain activity, or is there an immaterial mind state that activates the material brain state?

ever, scientific investigation of the characteristics relevant to causal interaction has been too restricted thus far to eliminate the possibility of such mind-brain interaction. What can be done is to examine and see if these supposed mental events do affect physical events. Psychosomatic (mind/body) medicine and

ESP research are two areas that have supplied evidence of such interaction. In a larger sense, who could not agree that man's mind states — his aspirations, fears, ideals, and longings — have had a significant part in the shaping of world history? To presume otherwise is unreasonable.

Of course, to accept the plausibility of the immaterial mind may involve changing one's concept of the physical universe — a concept that for most scientists has come from materialistic presuppositions and not from data alone. For example, it has been said that any mind-brain interaction would violate the conservation of energy principle, i.e., if a mind state started a brain state, then the brain would have gained kinetic energy from nowhere. This law is valid, however, only in a closed system. The ultimate question, in fact, that scientists face in the mind-brain problem is this: "Is the physical world a closed system, after all?" If it is open to nonphysical parameters, then mind-brain interaction ceases to be a problem.

Brain Function and the Mind

It has been suggested that the brain operates in much the same fashion as a computer, with various parts of the brain controlling behavioral and psychological phenomena. The motor cortex of the brain is involved in commands to the body for muscle movement; the visual cortex is involved with visual perception; the inner areas of the brain seem to mediate feelings of hunger, sex, thirst, aggression, etc. Behavioral and psychological processes function properly when billions of nerve cells in all areas are "firing" because of incoming sensory activity and when well-established associative connections exist between neurons. However, is the "mind's" thinking, fearing, and self-consciousness due only to billions of neurons active in certain patterns? Can it be categorically stated that the mind equals the brain state at a given moment?

Evidence is available to demonstrate that this materialistic model is not adequate to explain what is known about psychological experience. Recent brain research, which we will discuss later, particularly insists on the necessity of some sort of mind that tran-

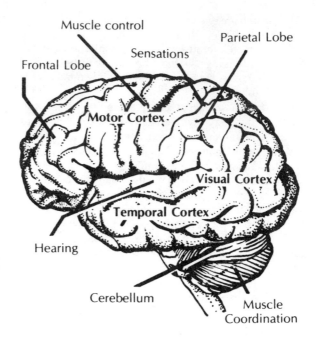

Muscle control

Parietal Lobe

Sensations

Frontal Lobe

Motor Cortex

Visual Cortex

Temporal Cortex

Hearing

Cerebellum

Muscle
Coordination

A schematic side view of the outside of the human brain indicating main divisions and some localized functions.

scends the physiology of the brain in order to explain self-consciousness.

Reductionism is a way of viewing man that reduces him to an explanation of his parts, i.e., man equals a collection of individual brain and body processes. But reductionism is unable to answer why the whole man seems to be more than the sum of his physical parts. Why is reading this paragraph more than electrical buzzing inside your skull? This problem must be faced on all levels of scientific inquiry.

For example, does increasing complexity of the right compounds in the right relationships explain the presence of life in a cell? Does increasing complexity of brain matter explain the presence of consciousness in animals and self-consciousness in man? When does a neural impulse traveling at a measurable speed become an image? Electrical currents in the brain either cause chemical changes or heat reactions, or set up electrical fields. Which of these is the image or the moral notion that we experience? There is nothing in the operational definition of the firing of neurons that could relate a wave of negative electrical potential to a conscious decision. In other words, brain events cannot adequately explain mind events. To say that brain function is more than the aggregate activities of all its neurons connotes some tangible addition. But, more of what? Mass? Electric charges? Dimensions? Surely, it is none of these. Then what? Perhaps some unfathomable, weightless, chargeless nonmaterial. Many scientific names have been invoked (vital principle, formative drive, etc.) for such an unknown. Might not *mind* be a simpler word?

Nor do relationships between the material parts of man's brain create the "more" that we see in his psychological makeup. Of course, a materialist, who denies the existence of the mind, could always sidestep the existence of mental qualities in man too because the simple addition of body and brain parts does not make up a thinking, feeling, self-conscious creature. (Remember that Frankenstein was only a science fiction character.) This is the reason that a materialist like the psychologist B. F. Skinner actually denies the existence of true psychological processes in man, and, in a sense, man himself. In his book *Beyond Freedom and Dignity* he says, "To man *qua* man we readily say good riddance,"[5] meaning that the man beyond the machine brain doesn't exist. The rugged naturalism of such a materialist has drawn a lot of praise. However, it makes little sense to deny the mind as a genuine dimension of man just to avoid suspicion that one is flirting with supernaturalism.

Electrical stimulation of the brains of conscious human patients suggests the presence of a mental awareness that transcends the level of brain activity. For example, during the course of brain surgery on patients suffering from epilepsy, Wilder Penfield (1956),[6] a famous neurophysiologist involved in the study of memory, conducted experiments in which he probed the temporal cortex of the brain with a weak electrical current. Each patient was under local anesthesia, fully conscious, and able to talk with Penfield.

Brain Stimulation and the Mind

They reported vivid memories of events or feelings in which they as the audience viewed themselves as actors, actually experiencing the past in these memories.

These patients were obviously experiencing two states simultaneously. The actual memory was a vivid psychological state brought forth by Penfield's probe; but it does not logically follow that the patients experienced two separate psychological states simultaneously, one of their present sensations in the operating room *and* the other the sensation of the past. Penfield's most recent book, *The Mystery of the Mind,* makes clear that he sides with the more probable idea that our being consists of two elements (brain and mind) rather than the less probable idea that our fundamental being rests on only brain. He says:

> For my own part, after years of striving to explain the mind on the basis of brain action alone, I have come to the conclusion that it is simpler (and far easier to be logical) if one adopts the hypothesis that our being does consist of two fundamental elements. . . . Because it seems to me certain that it will always be quite impossible to explain the mind on the basis of neuronal action within the brain, and because it seems to me that the mind develops and matures independently throughout an individual's life as though it were a continuing element, and because a computer (which the brain is) must be programmed and operated by an agency capable of independent understanding, I am forced to choose the proposition that our being is to be explained on the basis of two fundamental elements.[7]

In cancer patients the medical thalamus of the brain is often stimulated electrically because the resulting disruption of tissue there can give effective pain relief. In some patients such electrical stimulation produces extreme anxiety attacks, which one patient vividly described as "rather like the feeling of having just been missed by a car and leaped back to the curb and wept B-r-r-r."[8] Stimulation of other brain areas can cause some patients to feel emotion only in one side of the body. They report a "vital anxiety in the left chest." Does this mean that there were two minds existing because two neural states existed, one anxious and another not anxious? Certainly not. It seems more accurate to say that such emotional feelings are only generalized feelings of arousal. However, a rich emotional structure is formed, in partnership with the moral and social contexts of a person's mind. An experiment by Schacter and Singer (1962)[9] has well demonstrated that the observable physiology is not the prime mover of human emotional states. Subjects injected with adrenalin became euphoric when they were in a room with an actor who was faking euphoria, and they became angry when placed with an actor who was faking extreme anger. It is obvious from this that a study of human emotions and behavior requires first and foremost a study of the social contexts within which people move, and not just a study of their physiological states.

Who Observes Brain States?

If one takes the materialist's position and asserts that human awareness and experience are only the collective firings of billions of neurons, then there are some difficulties that he must answer. First of all, there is the enigma of equivalence of receptor function. All neurons are identical in their activity. The only difference between the firing of neurons in the visual cortex and the auditory cortex is, perhaps, in the rate and timing of neuron firing. Why, then, do we see in one case and hear in another? The neuron structure is the same, the physical activity is the same, and yet, there are different psychological experiences. For the materialist to propose the place theory (i.e., different locations of neurons in the brain give rise to different subjective experiences) is only *labeling,* not *explaining* the phenomenon.

Another problem with the materialist's view of man is that brain activity must be collected into output and then "known" at some point. A materialistic view of sensory experience and brain states sees the brain as a register of sensory data, much like a TV screen. Take the visual system, for example, where neurons in the optic nerve and visual pathways fire to certain visual images displayed on the retina in the back of the eye. Each neuron is sensitive to a particular location on the retina and, hence, a part of the visual field. Therefore, in the experience of seeing a chair, for example, various neurons respond to the various lines and colors as parts of the chair.[10] The cells combine their information to display images in the visual cortex in some way. So the brain could be compared to a TV screen in this case, with the final cells in the visual cortex displaying what the eye has seen, with small changes due to interference and amplification from memory and attentional brain areas. But the unanswered question is, Who is watching the TV screen in your head in order to know what all the final neurons are collectively reporting?

Visual scientists have suggested that this process of many individual cells feeding information to a fewer number of cells (which cells respond to more complicated images) ultimately gives the task of "seeing" complicated images to a very small number of cells.[11] It has been humorously hinted (by Lettvin et al.) that these final cells would have to be equivalent to a little green frog in every frog's brain in order to see what the big frog is looking at.[12]

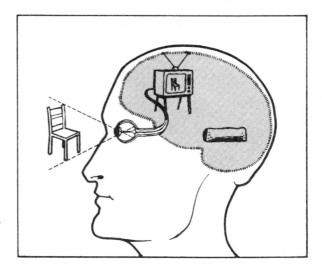

A materialistic view of sensory experience and brain states, depicting the brain as simply a register of sensory data, much like a TV screen.

But that is the problem. There are no little frogs in frog's brains or little men in human heads — only cells. If no one is at home in your head, there shouldn't be any experience at all. Thus, what began as a brilliant, vividly colored object, carefully registered on the retina and transmitted with wonderful precision to the inner visual cortex would there terminate by fizzle! It has the irony of a flop on opening night. If a computer prints out in an empty room, what experience is there in the absence of a knower? This concept of a knower, and the distinction between subject and object, cannot be dismissed, since it is one of the basic presuppositions of all types of knowledge. To make man the mere register of events is to leave unsolved the problem of self-conscious experience (the self being the "you" that gives experience to brain states). To use the title of Koestler's book (1967), there appears to be a "ghost in the [man] machine."[13]

Karl Pribram, a famous neurophysiologist, discusses this in his book *Languages of the Brain*. He says:

> Images and feelings are ghosts — but they are ghosts that inhabit my own and my patients' subjective worlds. They are our constant companions and I want to explain them.

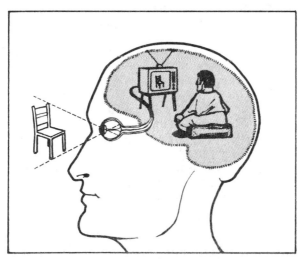

Another look at the brain, illustrating the self-conscious experience, which presupposes the presence of a "knower."

They reside "in" that machine yet they cannot be pointed at. If we ignore them, all we have is a behaving machine. I am interested in the ghosts, the psychological functions — not just the machine brain. . . .[14]

Debate continues over what parapsychologists (ESP researchers) have shown or have not shown. Yet, the problem of accepting their work as scientific stems not from their methods or controls, but from the current scientific presupposition that the immaterial mind does not exist and is not a factor in material events. But, unless there is a gigantic conspiracy in university departments all over the world, there does appear to exist a small number of individuals who obtain knowledge existing in other people's minds. This is obviously not the normal brain-to-mouth-to-ear-to-brain communication. Even in the Soviet Union, where the existence of the immaterial mind might be considered heresy, serious ESP research is blossoming.

Mental communication does not appear to follow known physical laws such as the inverse square law (i.e., ESP works as well over long distances as short distances), prompting scientists to investigate the laws of the immaterial mind. This is not to say that all the ESP research in the world is important or even valid; nevertheless, many good scientists consider it true that the physical comprises only a *portion* of reality, especially when one is dealing with human beings and the mind.

Physics is another discipline in which the traditional materialistic approach to man and things is making room for a larger view. Warner Heisenberg, one of the giants of quantum physics, is best remembered for his celebrated Principle of Indeterminacy, which seriously questioned causal determinism in physics. Heisenberg has repeatedly emphasized that atoms are not things. One cannot accurately describe electrons, which form the atom's outer shell, by the traditional concepts of location, velocity, energy, and size. At the atomic level the objective world in space and time no longer exists.

Consider neutrinos, elementary particles that are truly ghostlike: they have no mass, no electric charge, and no magnetic field; they are not attracted by gravity, nor captured or repelled by electric and magnetic fields. And yet they exist. Strict presuppositions like "whatever lacks measurable mass does not exist" would eliminate a genuine portion of reality in current physics! In the same way, strict materialistic pre-suppositions about man and the immaterial mind have boxed psychology into a narrow view of the nature of man.

Another area of knowledge that speaks about the immaterial part of man is religious authority. A scientist must not be lured into thinking that scientific enterprise is the only successful avenue for acquiring knowledge. Very few of the major questions in life can even be investigated scientifically, since strict scientific method demands replication in experimentations.

Judeo-Christian biblical documents discuss the existence of the soul of man (the word *soul* in Hebrew and Greek being comparable to the word *mind*). The truth of these documents depends on the claim that God exists, knows about such things, and has spoken to man about them; and that one can in some way validate the authority of these recorded words and guarantee that the records have survived history intact. This, of course, is the impetus behind many Christian scholars who have gathered a considerable amount of evidence for fulfilled biblical prophecies, miracles, the resurrection of Christ, and the survival of the original biblical text (Wilson, 1977; McDowell, 1972; Pinnock, 1971; Ramm, 1953).[15] The point to be made is that millions of human beings believe in the existence of the immaterial soul or mind, not just from individual, unverifiable experience, but from a reliable authoritative source, one that invites the scrutiny of the scientist. This information is equally available to the psychologist as an area for rigorous inquiry, which could serve the purpose of freeing him from his present limited starting point in the study of man.

In summary, it seems more reasonable to accept the notion of the mind than to insist on understanding man as a neurological computer. Not only does this view fit what is known about human experience and the attributes of the physical brain, but it appears as if the only resistance to believing in the immaterial mind comes from presuppositions in psychology about what can be studied and what consequently can be shown to exist. Even these presuppositions are changing in the laboratory of the parapsychologist and the physicist.

Within psychology itself the mood is also changing among some psychologists, notably cognitive and humanistic psychologists. The field of humanistic psychology, while often failing to shake entirely free of the presuppositions of the materialist and the evolutionist, has nevertheless refused to deal with man on a material level alone, as seen in the work of Gordon Allport,[16] Viktor Frankl,[17] Rollo May,[18] Eric Fromm,[19] Abraham Maslow,[20] and others. It fits the facts to believe in the immaterial part of man, and furthermore, it is irrational to affirm that the immaterial does not exist, when science, by its own definition cannot study such things. Sir John Eccles, Nobel Prize winner in brain physiology, verges on the answer:

> I can explain my body and my brain, but there's something more: I can't explain my own existence. What makes me a unique being?[21]

Is Man's Behavior Determined?

Chapter Abstract

Belief that brain action is the source of all human behavior is shown to have spawned the theory that human behavior is never the result of choice, only determined by the triggering of biological processes. Explanations of man's behavior from such cause-and-effect experiments on animals are shown to ignore man's unique sense of "self," of responsibility, of truth, and of achievement.

Is Man's Behavior Determined?

Determinism is a belief that a man's behavior is inevitable, and any sense of freedom is therefore an illusion. This view depends on the presupposition that every effect has a material cause, and such causes are incompatible with free will.

For example, consider the case of a man writing. Why does he write? Determinism says that finger, arm, and body muscles act in putting him through the behavioral performance. The muscles are activated by nerves, and nerves are stimulated by chemical interactions, etc. Every preparatory act is caused; therefore, the writer is determined. Even in his choice of words, complex but determined physiological states not only produce his words but also give him the feeling of freedom in the whole process. If determinism is true, then both those who argue for and those who argue against determinism are determined. This is a rather strange state of affairs. Do atoms argue over determinism, or do men?

The Essence of
Human Nature

Material Cause
and Free Will

The first question to be explored in dealing with determinism is this: Are material cause and free will incompatible? The answer is that personal freedom and laws of causation do not have to be incompatible. Consider that a scientific law is a statement of certain patterns of events, such as the regular falling of apples in accordance with gravitation. Law is not a description of the force making apples fall nor a final explanation of why all the apples fall; rather, it is a description of events. In the same way, scientists construct laws, physical and psychological, that describe man's behavior but that are not very likely the whole or real cause. Such laws only describe the pattern of events in human behavior. As was said earlier, nothing in the firing of a neuron can explain a conscious decision. For those who believe in freedom, it is legitimate to say that a man raised his arm because he had a "reason" to do so and at the same time to describe all the physical causes of arm raising. To be able to predict that a man will raise his arm does not preclude his option to have acted otherwise.

It is important to realize that we do not want to use the word *freedom* to mean "unpredictability." Freedom is self-determinism. Freedom, far from abandoning the properties of cause and effect (predictability, structure, organization), possesses the additional property of flexibility. Freedom without cause would be a nightmare in which no one could understand or count on the behavior of others. Freedom is superimposed upon a structured, physical world, not used in place of it. There is compatibility.

Such descriptions of free will operating in a material, caused world are usually rejected on the basis of reductionistic thought. As mentioned before, reductionism states that the whole is equal to the sum of the parts, or that man can be totally defined by a description of his physiochemical parts. This view denies that complex configurations of matter, such as man, may have characteristics that are not contained within the sum of the parts considered separately. Reductionistic thought colors the study of biology, psychology, sociology, political science, etc. These fields are ultimately based on matter and the atomic particles that compose it. Many therefore assume that behavior is reducible to physics. However, as one views higher levels of interaction, new and unique characteristics appear that are irreducible to the lower levels that form the material foundation. A chimpanzee swinging on a rotten tree vine would mean one thing to an animal psychologist, and quite another to the physicist studying the same event on the level of atomic particles. Likewise, a person may feel and act freely, while at the same time a physicist may describe to him all the mechanics of his behavior. The physicist may declare that human freedom does not exist on the basis of his physical description. However, when he does so, he is sharpening the detail under his microscope, while losing sight of the larger picture of man.

B. F. Skinner, famous Harvard psychologist, has popularized a model of determinism in man's behavior both by his year of experimentation on rats and by two of his books — *Walden Two*[22] and *Beyond Freedom and Dignity*.[23] Behaviorism is that branch of psychology that seeks to establish a cause-effect correlation between behavior features of the environment. Behavior, thus predicated upon particular stimuli in the environment, is treated as a response to that environment. Therefore, behaviorists talk in terms of stimulus-response theories of learning. Skinner has made popular the technique of operant conditioning in the famed "Skinner's box." Here, in this highly controlled environment, it can be shown that a behavior followed by a suitable reward (reinforcement) is likely to be repeated. It is not difficult to see where some behaviorists like Skinner begin to deny free will in man when their data are coupled with their presupposition of materialism. All that such a behaviorist can observe in the experience of man are rewards stimulating the occurrence of behaviors. Skinner's views have led him to conclude that man is only a machine controlled by the rewarding and punishing features of his environment. In *Beyond Freedom and Dignity,* he says:

Personal exemption from a complete determinism is revoked as scientific analysis progresses, particularly in accounting for the behavior of the individual.[24]

A close look will show that not all of man's behavior fits the materialistic model — and so much so that it is reasonable to reject such a strict deterministic view of man as out of step with observed reality. The following sections will consider some physiological and psychological objections to Skinner's view of determinism in man.

Brain Research

The brain seems to be roughly divided into areas that have specific functions in motor, sensory, and affective behavior. Information on brain area function is available to neurophysiologists because of experiments in which various areas of the brain are stimulated or damaged, electrically or chemically, and observations are then made of the behavior of the organism to judge what that specific area of the brain was involved with.

Electrical stimulation of a certain area of motor cortex in a monkey could produce an eye blink in a very mechanical fashion. It appears that the experimenter is pushing a switch in the computer-brain of the monkey and the monkey moves, sometimes in very complicated sequences.[25] Hoebel and Teitelbaum (1962)[26] reported similar findings of mechanical behavior after the destruction of certain brain areas in rats. Lesions or injuries in the ventral medial hypothalamus of rats produced hyperphagia, a condition in which the rats ate voraciously and continually, gaining two or three times their body weight, apparently like little machines out of control.

Perhaps the most stunning experiments have come from the laboratory of José Delgado. In one filmed experiment Delgado fights a ferocious bull in a bull ring.[27] The bull has had an electrode planted in his brain for the purpose of controlling his aggressive feelings, and Delgado holds a wireless transmitter to enable him to stimulate the bull's brain. In the film, the bull charges Delgado and then stops his attack whenever the electrode is activated. Again, these experiments attempt to show the mechanical nature of animal behavior and, of course, of people also by

43

Is Man's Behavior Determined?

Delgado "fights" an aggressive bull with electrode brain control.

The bull does not become peaceful after electrode shock.

The shock appears to leave the bull only stunned and confused.

generalization from this animal research. This is the theme picked up by the popular novel *The Terminal Man,* cited in the introduction.

Since people do not have electrodes in their brains, what, then, would a determinist say controls man's behavior? The behaviorist suggests that the environment is the controller. External and internal stimuli: sights, sounds, memories, blood content, etc., all trigger in complex ways the behavior of man. Gazing at a hamburger stimulates the hunger area of the brain and a person thinks and acts appropriately, much as a garbage disposal acts appropriately when it is turned on. The behaviorist also points out that man actually *feels* out of control in many of his appetites, such as sex or hunger, because he *is* beyond his own control. The terminology of "turning on" sexually is especially appropriate in this context. What has the supporter of free will to say to all this scientific data?

It is not valid to defend animal free will in every case. Spiders have no brains and are therefore automatons. Monkeys with brains probably experience some free choice. But the real question is man. First there needs to be a closer examination of the brain-research data on the animals just discussed, which examination will show that it is not necessarily the absence of free will in animals that is being demonstrated.

**Fat Rats and
Mad Bulls**

Elliot Valenstein, professor of psychology and neuroscience at the University of Michigan, discusses in his book *Brain Control* the misleading interpretation about hyperphagic rats.

> Anyone observing an animal suddenly picking up a pellet of food immediately after the stimulation has been turned up and then continuing to gorge itself until the stimulation has been turned off cannot help but form the impression of a tremendous control that can be exerted by brain stimulation. These first impressions can be very misleading, as can be the extrapolations from these examples to human clinical problem. . . . The impression exists that if electrodes are placed in a specific part of the brain, a particular behavior can inevitably be evoked. Those who have participated in this research know that this is definitely not the case.[28]

*Lesions were made
on this rat's hypo-
thalamus. As a result,
it gorged itself, like a
machine out of con-
trol, to three or four
times its normal
weight.*

Valenstein goes on to say that when the rats were
presented with different types of food, they would stop
eating or begin drinking. Obviously, something more
is involved with Delgado's bull, which, when stimulated in the brain, did not stop "dead" and become
docile. As the film shows, the bull stopped and whirled
around viciously in a clockwise fashion each time the
stimulation began. Delgado explains this movement of
the bull as a "motor effect."[29] It is more likely that the
bull was stunned and confused, rather than no longer
aggressive. The idea that we have control of an aggressive or hunger area of the brain is far too simple a
concept to explain human and animal behavior. If
someone punched you in the nose and made you furi-
ous, he shouldn't claim to have located your aggres-

sive area. So these experiments have not demonstrated the type of control over animals necessary to rule out the existence of free choice.

A Difference Between Free Will and Brain States

These same types of brain control experiments can be observed in human subjects with similar, misleading results. For example, after a particular type of brain surgery, some patients eat considerably more than normal, much like hyperphagic rats. Karl Pribram (1971) discusses one such female patient who gained one hundred pounds in the year after surgery. What is interesting is that she never reported feelings of hunger; but in the presence of food she ate voraciously.[30]

This patient's mental state concerning hunger was not involved, but she seemed biologically impaired — an impairment that was accompanied by excessive eating. There is a clear distinction between her mind set and her behavior. It is logical to expect that her free will, a function of the mind, is observed with difficulty because her brain — the material through which her mind works — is damaged in some way. The same would be true of a cripple in a wheelchair. His inability to control his body because of neural damage does not mean that he has no free will.

Another example of the tension between human free will and a brain state is seen in a human experiment similar to that of Delgado and the bull. King (1961) describes a woman who had electrodes implanted for epilepsy and was observed when her amygdala was stimulated. The stimulation would supposedly cause her to become aggressive. This is what she said when the stimulation began: "I feel like I want to get up from this chair! Please don't let me do it! Don't do this to me. I don't want to be mean!"[31]

It is important to notice that she felt like being mean, but she did not give in and did not strike out. She resisted the implanted electrode with a display of moral and social notions. It has been suggested that other social and moral brain areas are involved here as part of the determinants. But to say there is a social or moral area that is equivalent to what human beings exhibit morally or socially is a naive approach to brain activity. The aggressive area of the woman's brain brought forth only generalized feelings, not instructions to attack. In addition, if one wants to propose new brain areas for every human behavior or experience, the brain would soon be so large that it would not fit within the boundaries of the galaxy!

No, the mechanical view of brain activity simply cannot adequately explain all the data. The more plausible view is that human behavior is *influenced* by brain states but that the immaterial mind that transcends these states gives freedom to direct conscious human behavior.

**Psychological
Objections
to Determinism**

The first psychological objection to determinism in man is that a purely neuronal or chemical view of human activity ignores the evidence for the "self" as one of the influences on human behavior. The self in psychology refers to a person's mind and to that person as a whole person.

The power of self and self-concept overriding environmental influences is seen in studies of self-fulfilling prophecy. For example, it has been shown that students get better grades when they believe their grades depend on circumstances within their control (internal locus of control) rather than circumstances outside their control (external locus of control).[32] Thus a student fulfills his own "prophecies." It has been argued that the self is made up of past experiences and internal states and so it, too, is determined. However, this view of the self is the result of materialistic presuppositions. Undoubtedly, the self is in part *influenced* by environment, but there is no reason to reduce it to a *mere product* of the environment. There is every reason to believe that the mental concepts of desire shape the course of individual history.

There is another weakness in the behaviorist view that seeks to explain all human behavior as controlled ultimately by some physical reward called a "primary reinforcer." Obviously, activities like attending class or writing a paper are done with no food pellet waiting at the end. The theorist view is the concept of secondary reinforcement, where a nonphysically rewarding stimulus can become effective when it has been associated with a primary reinforcer. For example, food will motivate an animal to work at some task, and plastic money that can be exchanged for bananas soon becomes *reinforcing* for monkey subjects. The "worthless" money becomes reinforcing in the context of a genuine physiological reward. In the same way, man, according to the behaviorist, earns money or works for grades; food is on the other end. Or he talks in a certain way and grooms himself; sex is nearby.

However, to reduce human motivation to secondary reinforcement or endless higher chains is impossible. What is the chain of higher level reinforcers that explains what word a poet will choose next, or all the steps involved in that first giant step on the moon? What about all the behavior that never finds physical reward or even braves certain punishment? As with the loser at the slot machine, there has to be a payoff sometime, or the behavior stops! Yet, man's behavior goes on and on, far beyond what the concept of primary and secondary reinforcement will allow.

It is also necessary for the behaviorist to explain the apparent exceptions to environmental determinism. Why are some behaviors expressed in spite of the conditioning environment, such as the behavior of Aleksandr Solzhenitsyn in communist Russia? And why do criminals come from both bad and good environments at about the same rate? Why, in the light of determinism, is there white collar crime? If the environment is solely responsible, one would expect conditioning to work in society as well as it does in the rat lab. It has been argued that there are just some conditions in Solzhenitsyn's life that we aren't aware of, but that have nevertheless been the major shaping influences on his life and views. This is the "hidden parameters" argument, we are told. One can see all the major influences in his life except the ones that are necessary to explain his behavior! With this type of argument it is impossible for determinism to be refuted, because the determinist is retreating into his faith presupposition and not being honest with the data before him.

Another difficulty with determinism is that it does not make sense on the level where we live our lives. It is existentially repugnant. Consider science. Scientific behavior to the determinist would not be considered deliberate activity but the result of previous environmental causes. Results in the laboratory would no longer be dependent on "truth," but rather on circumstances surrounding the researchers. Even B. F. Skinner's papers on determinism would be a product of environmental forces in his life and bear only an accidental relation to truth, if any at all. Determinism makes the ideas of truth and human responsibility devoid of meaning.

And yet, even Skinner does not fail to assume the existence of truth as he teaches, or responsibility as he organizes his life, spends his salary, etc. How can anyone explain the phenomenal success of science if even its activity is caused by an unpredictable environment? To summarize this section on determinism, there is a good case to be made for free will in man. In fact, if there were no evidence for free will at all, it would still be difficult to be a consistent determinist, let alone to live like one.

Is Man an Animal?

Chapter Abstract

An evaluation is made of recent attempts to teach different kinds of languages to chimpanzees and the resultant uncertainty about man's linguistic distinctiveness. A closer study shows a definite difference in language usage, particularly regarding concept formation and language acquisition. Other distinctions considered include man's unique use of technology, culture, worship, and moral notions.

Is Man an Animal?

It is obvious that there can be no denial of the similarities between some animal bodies and the human anatomy and physiology. It should also be admitted that it is quite probable that some animals are not mere biological machines. While a brainless amoeba is easily seen as an automaton, it is very difficult to put chimpanzees in the same category. However, throughout the history of thought there has always been recognized a massive gap between man and even the highest of animals.

Man stands alone in so many tangible ways that one can reasonably suggest that man is not just an animal. A glance at man's behavior confirms that he is self-conscious, has complex motivation and purpose, and transcends his present moment in time. Attempts to demonstrate the same of animal behavior are hard pressed to show anything more than conscious intelligence of largely present physiological purpose, i.e., not removed from self, matter, or present tense.   53

Consider the brain and its learned neural pathways as equipment that men and higher animals use: how well, for what purpose, and in what ways are animals motivated in using this equipment? This section will consider the distinctions between man and higher animals primarily in the area of concept formation and language because this area is the clearest evidence of man's internal nature. We will briefly examine other behavioral differences, as well, such as man's use of technology, culture, worship, and his moral notions — all of which suggest a true distinction between man and animals.

The Question of Language

Scientists have said that if there is any distinction between man and animal, it is in man's use of language and conceptual thought. This distinction has been blurred recently by attempts to teach language to chimpanzees in many animal laboratories. It has been suggested that if these primates had conceptual thoughts, no one would ever know, because they lack most of the anatomical features of vocal apparatus necessary for speaking.

Hayes (1951) reports being able to teach a chimp named Vikki four words, like "cup" or "mama," which Vikki could repeat only while holding her lips.[33] This anatomical barrier has been circumvented by recent researchers (Gardner & Gardner, 1969; Premack, 1970, 1971).[34] The Gardners, for example, taught their subject, Washoe, to use American sign language signals for the deaf, which signs she often used even spontaneously and in combinations. Premack used plastic and metal objects of various shapes on a magnetic display board. These shapes, called "words," could be manipulated by Sarah, his chimpanzee subject. In response to food rewards, Sarah learned to place these "words" in proper, meaningful sentence structure — for example, "Mary give apple Sarah." Premack even used a symbol for a question mark and "asked" Sarah about the sameness or difference of two test objects. A grandiose interpretation of all this research appeared on the cover of *Psychology Today* (Jan. 1974) where the question is asked,

"Proud of communicating? Don't look back. There's an ape gaining on you."

But a closer examination of language in chimps must question such an interpretation of the data. To say that these animals are truly using language is going beyond the experimental results at this point. While everyone knows what was in the mind of the experimenter as he taught the chimps to manipulate plastic blocks, the real question is, What was in the minds of the chimps as they used the signs, and were they demonstrating true language usage?

A chimpanzee learns to give the correct sign for "book," but does this demonstrate that animals have self-reflective thought?

Man has self-reflective thought, i.e., the ability to analyze his conscious experience and to use it as a source of abstract knowledge. The absence of self-reflective thought should restrict subhuman species to rely exclusively on concrete signs, which lack some of the characteristics of genuine symbols.

In human speech, words are genuine symbols (many of which are detached from physical representations) transmitted through a grammatical structure. Animal signs such as the hand signs of Washoe are not true concepts, since a physical representation is always involved. A true concept, such as the meaning of the words "political science," could not be grasped by Washoe through any physical representation.

One must not mistake animal knowledge in terms of visual experiences and concrete imagery with true concepts. It is true that rats have been conditioned to respond to triangularity in several forms as an example of generalization of stimuli. Something similar to abstraction takes place because the animal is able to isolate certain sensory qualities of the stimulus object. But this cannot be equated with human abstractions in language. In spite of the fact that Sarah mastered all the operations required of her in the laboratory, the plastic "words" represent not true concepts but only sensory abstractions. In sensation an organism will respond to a variety of relationships between objects. However, mere response to relationships doesn't indicate a recognition of them as relationships.

In fact, Sarah and other chimps "learn" language by being conditioned to associate an entire series of concrete signs in a fixed manner. Similarly, a rat can learn a complex behavior pattern by learning the individual elements of the pattern, one at a time, and this will result in a type of chain-link behavior sequence. A pigeon can learn to play a song on a piano, one note at a time, by this method called "chaining." No one would suggest that the pigeon has a grasp of the melody. Has Sarah learned any differently? True human use of grammar involves a "theory of language" that enables a person to understand the meaning of millions of possible sentence structures that he has never confronted before.

The Acquisition of Language

A good example of the symbolic imagination and intelligence of man exhibited in language can be found in the classic case of Helen Keller as a blind, deaf-mute child. Mrs. Sullivan, Helen's teacher, spoke of the time when the young child began to understand the meaning and function of language:

> I must write you a line this morning because something very important has happened. Helen has taken the second great step in her education. She has learned that everything has a name, and that the manual alphabet is the key to everything she wants to know.
>   . . . . This morning, while she was washing, she wanted to know the name for "water." When she wants to know the name of anything, she points to it and pats my

hand. I spelled "w-a-t-e-r" and thought no more about it until after breakfast. . . . [Later on] we went out to the pump house, and I made Helen hold her mug under the spout while I pumped. As the cold water gushed forth, filling the mug, I spelled "w-a-t-e-r" in Helen's free hand. The word coming so close upon the sensation of cold water rushing over her hand seemed to startle her. She dropped the mug and stood as one transfixed. A new light came into her face. She spelled "water" several times. Then she dropped on the ground and asked for its name and pointed to the pump and the trellis and suddenly turning around she asked for my name. I spelled "teacher." All the way back to the house she was highly excited, and learned the name of every object she touched, so that she added thirty new words to her vocabulary. The next morning she got up like a radiant fairy. She has flitted from object to object, asking the name of everything and kissing me for very gladness . . . everything must have a name now. Wherever we go, she asks eagerly for the names of things she has not learned at home. She is anxious for her friends to spell, and eager to teach the letters to everyone she meets. She drops the signs and pantomime she used before, as soon as she has words to supply their place, and the acquirement of a new word affords her the liveliest pleasure. And we notice that her face grows more expressive each day.[35]

What an excellent example Helen Keller gave of a human mind that could use the simplest tools available to express itself.

It is also very clear that human beings do not acquire language in the same way that chimps are taught to use signs. There are two views on the origin and nature of human language: the empiricist view and the rationalist view. The empiricists believe that language is simply a learned or acquired response and that any creature with a high ability to learn could learn language. The rationalist view says that man has an inborn capability for language, making him qualitatively different from the animals. The weight of the evidence lies with the latter view.[36]

The uniformity of language acquisition among men fits perfectly with the rationalist position. Careful studies of the most primitive societies reveal that their languages are always exceedingly complex. In addition, no people are ever without a language, except children of extreme mental deficiency or children who have been totally isolated from language use. If language acquisition depended primarily on the training a child receives, one would expect differences in training to correlate with differences in language acquisition. However, all children learn a full-blown linguistic system despite variations in the amount of speech they are exposed to.

In addition, humans acquire language in a relatively perfect fashion regardless of their intelligence level, suggesting an innate linguistic capacity. In various academic areas bright children do better than less-bright children, and some children even "fail" to learn. But this is not so in language. All children, even those of low intelligence, learn to talk in ways virtually identical to their respective models. Every child masters the complex set of rules of grammar that specify an infinite set of possible sentences. This is an amazing feat, since the child masters it on the basis of indirect and fragmentary evidence, and at an age when he is hardly attempting a great deal of logical, analytical thought. This is the reason that Noam Chomsky, a linguist from MIT, argued against B. F. Skinner's view of language acquisition, which is in terms of instrumental learning.[37]

Given the high level of chimpanzee intelligence and the suitability of using chimpanzees in learning situations, one would expect them to succeed in true language use to a degree proportional to their intelligence and to demonstrate in the wild at least rudiments of language. Experiments and careful natural observation have shown that this is not the case. When man gave the chimps the technique to express themselves, it was discovered that they had nothing to say.

In addition to language, we can observe other behaviors unique to man that are well within the capacities of animal intelligence. Again it is the unique human mind and the ability of self-conscious thought that bequeaths greater capacities to man, capacities such as his expanded purpose in life and his expanded world awareness.

It is evident that some animals are able to make and use simple tools. Why is it, then, that tool usage is virtually absent in the entire animal kingdom? A polar bear will club a seal with an icicle now and then; a monkey can throw rocks and use sticks to knock down bananas — but he will rarely do so. Even when taught in experimental labs, animals are persistent in the use of tools only when consistently rewarded. Subhuman primates live today exactly as they did thousands of years ago — no progress, no change. The reason for lack of advancement among primates in the use of tools or other constructions is that they lack motivation and purpose, a sense of self, a sense of time, and a sense of order and form, all of which are dependent on self-conscious thought.

Man, wherever we find him, is a tool maker and tool user. He has built massive civilizations all over the earth and has been to the moon and back. He alone is

Expanded Purpose of Man

Man's expanded purpose is vividly illustrated by his journey to the moon. Sophisticated tool usage, building on past wisdom, and the pursuit of truth, all necessary prerequisites to the moon shots, are but several behaviors never seen in animals.

cultural in the sense that he preserves his intellectual accomplishments for the future and builds upon past wisdom. His sense of order and form results in art — the pursuit of beauty; and science — the pursuit of truth.

Man's expanded purpose is also seen in his varied

life style, in contrast to the life patterns in the animal world. While animals generally restrict themselves to one or two types of food, man eats everything under the sun. His body needs only several basic foods, and the stomach sends no complex signals to inspire the exotic recipes that enter the mind of man. In the same vein, man is the only creature who chooses to adorn his body. Exposure to the elements makes clothing necessary, but what except the mind of man provokes the heights of changing fashion, and the environmentally useless cosmetics and trinkets?

**Expanded
Awareness**

Man is the only creature on the globe with a sense and fear of death. Animals may struggle to live, but there is no indication that they fear death. Canadian anthropologist Dr. Arthur Custance discussed evidence for this assertion:

> One of the strongest evidences of the truth of this has resulted from the labors of Walt Disney's co-workers in their endeavor to photograph Nature, without upsetting it in the process. Extensive photographs have been taken of lions hunting their prey, in which the apparent fright of a herd is much more probably a kind of expression of animal energy, the sheer delight of violent muscular activity, the absence of real fear being evident from two facts: the first being that the herd stops its flight instantly and resumes nonchalant feeding the moment flight is no longer necessary, and the second being that the animals nearest to the creature captured by the predator show no concern whatever in its fate. It is generally agreed that loss of appetite is a genuine evidence of fear. That such animals should halt their flight and return at once to grazing suggests the total absence of fear in the ordinary sense. And that those who escaped should show no interest in the fate of the one which did not, even though the lion may be eating it in their presence, seems to demonstrate the complete absence of anticipation of death.[38]

In addition, it is only man who thinks of burying his dead. This is true even from the dawn of his history. In the Shanidar cave in Iraq were found several Neanderthal bodies buried on beds of eight different flowers and soft branches.[39] Other Neanderthal bodies in France are painted with ocher and adorned with collars and arm rings. The Neanderthal people therefore, confronted death ritualistically and with concern.

Moreover, examples of altruism and love are found in all humans, even in prehistoric settings. In the same Shanidar cave of Iraq, for example, was found a skeleton of a Neanderthal adult male who had probably been blind and had had one arm amputated early in life. He was about forty when he died and certainly was incapable of caring for himself all those years. Others "cared" for him. Small fur-lined sandals were also found, hinting a loving concern for the youngest members of this community.

Another dimension of man's expanded awareness is evidenced in his being burdened by moral tensions as he deals with others in his life. All across the globe and for all recorded time, he has had moral frameworks of some sort. These frameworks show that man's mind resists the stimulus demands of his environment or body when they oppose some organized or internalized code of morality. These moral notions are not exactly the same from culture to culture, but man is never without them. To think that moral tension could develop within a purely material and determined creature is incredible.

Finally, the practice of worship is unique to man. Everywhere man is found on his knees, reflecting an awareness both of self and of someone unseen and larger than self. Animals may howl at the moon and tremble before thunder and acquire superstitious behavior, but man displays a reverence of the unseen or an inner awareness that it exists. Man's intelligent worship has defied the category of superstition. Often it is said that man postulated a deity to explain things he otherwise couldn't understand, such as thunder. However, men who have closed these gaps in understanding continue to worship. This worship not only points to his conceptual grasp of deity, but also to his feelings that he was meant to relate to that deity as well as to people and to things.

What Then Can We Conclude?

Chapter Abstract

The presuppositions of man's strict materialism are based not on empirical evidence (which cannot prove or disprove the immaterial) but on denial by prebelief. The theory of spontaneous emergence of man's distinct qualities is considered but found insubstantial. More substance is claimed for an older view of a Creator revealing to man, who is his creation, a purpose for his uniqueness.

What Then Can We Conclude?

To answer every question on the nature of man and to lay to rest every wrong theory is not my purpose in this brief treatment. But, this look at several key issues in psychology on the nature of man consistently supports a view that man is not mere material, mechanical, or animal.

As was seen, strict materialistic views of man that ignore the mind come into conflict with recent brain research such as that of Wilder Penfield, which shows a simultaneous double consciousness in human beings. If one of these consciousnesses is the brain state, whence comes the other that is conscious of the first? Secondly, the nature of brain activity, as illustrated by the visual system, shows the need for the self or the mind at the end of the information processing system in the brain to give rise to our awareness of reality.

At this point it is reasonable to talk about dualistic theories of human nature (mind in a body), or the Hebrew-Christian model, which speaks of the material 65 (body) and immaterial (soul and spirit) parts of man as though these are thoroughly integrated into one functioning unit. The latter view seems to better fit current research on the brain, research that definitely shows an almost inseparable relationship between brain and mind function.

The question of animal "minds" has not been resolved, and more research is needed in this area. It is quite possible that some animals with well-developed brains have minds in which the mind state is a direct product of the brain state, or if not a brain by-product, the animal mind is not of the same "kind" as the human mind. The lack of evidence for self-consciousness in the animal points to an epiphenomenal (the incapability of consciousness to exert an influence on brain processes) mind, while the distinctiveness of human culture, language, sexuality, etc., points to a different type of innate capacity in the human mind.

Questions about determinism in man seem to face the same outcome as those on the existence of the mind because the two issues are integrally related. It is important to remember that neither free will nor determinism can be empirically demonstrated in man, since the scientific method presupposes the mechanical nature of things — which is assuming the very thing to be proved. This type of presuppositional argument is raised against the human experience of free choice by strict determinists because they deny the validity of the human mind and its faculties, and hence the independence of thought. It should be carefully noted that this is not *evidence* against free will, but a *denial* by *pre-belief*. In addition, the many examples of human subjects rejecting the promptings of the implanted brain electrodes appears to reduce any discussion of determinants to the level of influences. One could argue that he could plant a million electrodes in the human brain and control a person. However, this no more invalidates free will than does bending someone's arm behind his back to force his body into some behavior. Finally, psychological determinism is self-defeating because it ultimately refutes the validity of the very point it attempts to make. This was noted

> Determinism asserts that everything man does, thinks, or believes is determined by forces beyond his control. If a man believes something, he had to believe it. If he does something, he had to do it. If this is true, it follows that no knowledge or understanding of objective reality is possible to man. . . . If no knowledge is possible, then by what right and by what standard can the determinist claim any validity for his conclusions?[40]

When we consider man's relationship to the animal, we need to admit the force of our observations of man's distinctive culture, technology, and language. Often such clear data has been de-emphasized in the interest of preserving the biological explanations of man.

Man's unique capabilities are impossible to explain by any purely biological theory. The theory of evolution, for example, would predict gradually reduced versions of all man's abilities in the animal forms below him on the phylogenetic tree of life. However, there is no gradual transition from animals to man. So obvious are the discontinuities with regard to thought and personality in the proposed evolutionary sequence that some scientists and philosophers have proposed that these unique capabilities have spontaneously emerged from matter. But, if there is a biological mechanism that can account for the emergence of capabilities like self-conscious thought, it has eluded our search.

Beliefs that are held in spite of scientific observations can be a disservice to science, especially in the study of man. So often, in the name of science, men have condemned notions of the immaterial or free choice in man when in actuality the data support these very notions. Let us not be afraid to admit that man is more than science can measure. Dr. Gunther Stent in his article in *Science* entitled "Limits to the Scientific Understanding of Man" put it this way:

> But I think that it is important to give due recognition to this fundamental epistemological limitation to the human sciences, if only as a safeguard against the psychological or sociological prescription put forward by those who allege that they have already managed to gain a scientifically validated understanding of man.[41]

Finally, we should recognize debates on man's nature not just as academic exercises but as vital issues. At stake is our understanding of ourselves and our consequent well-being. If man is just material, mechanical, and animal, then life suddenly changes its meaning for those who have believed otherwise. Believing in the immaterial part of man allows one to believe intelligently in life after death and in an expanded purpose in this life.

A person's self-worth ultimately depends on a high view of the nature of man, for after all, if man is only biology, then why is his biology of any more worth than that of a cow or a tree? Why should we expect or strive for any high moral standard or qualities like kindness and mercy if man is nothing more than animal material and destined to evaporate with his body chemicals? This point was summarized very well by C. S. Lewis, the famous Cambridge University author, in his book *The Abolition of Man:*

> The real objection is that if man chooses to treat himself as raw material, raw material he will be: not raw material to be manipulated as he fondly imagined, by himself, but by mere appetite, that is, mere nature. . . .[42]

The materialistic, mechanical, and animal view of man, thus, is not only inadequate to explain man, but it is also destructive to him. In a world obstructed by an inadequate view of man and his problems, a fresh look at the nature of man is a most pressing need.

However, this author concludes that the more human nature is studied scientifically, the more apparent it becomes that the best description we have of man is not new at all. In fact, it is thousands of years old; and it is revelational, a disclosure by the Creator to His creation. The Christian view of man has long recognized the material and immaterial aspects to man's existence, his ability to make responsible and irresponsible choices, and the image of God[43] in his being. The Christian view also maintains that the ultimate description of the nature of man must be one that embraces his entire being and purpose. His physical nature must be properly related to the physical world if his needs are to be met; and, in the same way, his immaterial nature must be properly related to himself, his neighbor, and his Creator if his most essential needs are to be met. This is in good agreement with our psychological assessment of man.

Today, after all the scientific data has been discussed, we still declare with the psalmist:

> What is man, that thou art mindful of him? and the son of man, that thou visitest him? For thou hast made him a little lower than the angels, and hast crowned him with glory and honour.[44]

Response

MARTY J.
SCHMIDT

How much do scientists really know about the nature of man? Is the human mind nothing more than biological machinery that we can take apart and study — just as we might take apart a clock and examine its workings? Will science find a way to predict and control my thoughts in the same way that chemical reactions are predicted and controlled? Is man just another animal?

These questions both intrigue and trouble us, particularly when we read of startling recent developments in psychology and brain physiology. Indeed, much of the evidence seems to support a mechanical, deterministic view of man. Understandably, many people wonder if it is "unscientific" to believe in a spiritual side of man. Dr. Cosgrove's purpose in *The Essence of Human Nature* is to show that science and spirituality are not incompatible and that, if anything, laboratory data and scientific analysis affirm the presence of mind and human spirit.

Students in college psychology courses should find this book particularly interesting. Cosgrove reviews much of the research they have already encountered in their textbooks, including reports that pleasure, pain, and other physical drives can be controlled by delivering electrical impulses to specific brain sites, attempts to teach language to chimpanzees, and some of B. F. Skinner's work. However, this book addresses the vital issue that even the best textbooks seem to handle poorly or else avoid, namely, what do these studies really mean about the essence of human nature? After viewing the evidence, must we agree with Skinner that concepts such as mind and free will are simply illusions?

This book is especially valuable, I think, because it points out the limits of science in dealing with these issues. I am afraid that those of us who teach and research in psychology often mislead our students on the matter of what *is* known about man and what *can*

71

be known about man through scientific methods. We are prone to simplify issues and overinterpret data; we are reluctant to emphasize the limits and tentative nature of scientific proof. Perhaps we do so because we simply do not know better, or perhaps it is because we wish to enhance the importance of our research. Whatever the reason, the regrettable result is that scientific evidence is too easily equated with truth by many students and the general public. What is realized among scientists, but poorly communicated to the public, is that proof by scientific methods always includes the possibility of error. Moreover, there is a very big difference between research data and the interpretations of those data by the experimenters who produce them. It is perfectly reasonable, for instance, to admire the many important research findings of B. F. Skinner and yet disagree completely with his conclusions about determinism and behavior. As Cosgrove indicates, science has a particularly difficult time dealing with issues of free will vs. determinism, and the immaterial soul vs. the material brain, because science is necessarily limited to the study of physically determined processes and reductionistic explanations. It is not unscientific to recognize these limits.

I look forward to using this book in the classroom in conjunction with a standard textbook. The issues are of vital interest to many of the students who enroll in psychology courses every year, and the treatment here should stimulate productive discussion and thinking.

References

[1]Michael Crichton, *The Terminal Man* (New York: Bantam Books, 1973).

[2]John A. Wheeler, "The Universe as Home for Man," *American Scientist* 62 (1974): 685.

[3]Charles R. Darwin, *The Origin of Species* (London, 1859).

[4]Gustav Fechner, *Elements of Psychophysics,* Translated by H. E. Adler (New York: Holt, Rinehart and Winston, 1966).

[5]B. F. Skinner, *Beyond Freedom and Dignity* (New York: Alfred A. Knopf, 1971), p. 191.

[6]Wilder Penfield, "The Permanent Record of the Stream of Consciousness," *Acta Psychologica* 11 (1956): 47–69.

[7]Idem, *The Mystery of the Mind* (Princeton, N.J.: Princeton University Press, 1975), p. 80.

[8]José M. R. Delgado, *Physical Control of the Mind: Toward a Psychocivilized Society* (New York: Harper and Row, 1971), pp. 134–135.

[9]S. Schacter and J. Singer, "Cognitive, Social and Physiological Determinants of Emotional State," *Psychological Review* 69 (1962): 379–399.

[10]D. H. Hubel and T. N. Wiesel, "Receptive Fields, Binocular Interaction and Functional Architecture in the Cat's Visual Cortex" *Journal of Physiology* 160 (1962): 106–154; D. R. Brown, M. J. Schmidt, D. D. Fulgham, and M. P. Cosgrove, "Human Receptive Field Characteristics: Probe Analysis of Stabilized Images," *Vision Research* 13 (1973): 231–244.

[11]Peter C. Dodwell, *Visual Pattern Recognition* (New York: Holt, Rinehart and Winston, 1970).

[12]J. Y. Lettvin, H. R. Maturana, W. S. McCulloch and W. H. Pitts, "What the Frog's Eye Tells the Frog's Brain," *Proc. Inst. Radio Engineers* 47 (1959): 1941–1951.

[13]Arthur Koestler, *The Ghost in the Machine* (New York: Macmillan Co., 1967).

[14]Karl Pribram, *Languages of the Brain: Experimental Paradoxes and Principles in Neuropsychology* (Englewood Cliffs, N.J.: Prentice-Hall, 1971), pp. 100–1.

[15] Josh McDowell, *Evidence That Demands a Verdict* (San Bernadino, Calif.: Campus Crusade for Christ, 1972); Clark Pinnock, *Set Forth Your Case* (Chicago: Moody Press, 1971); Bernard Ramm, *Protestant Christian Evidences* (Chicago: Moody Press, 1953); Clifford A. Wilson, *Rocks, Relics, and Biblical Reliability* (Grand Rapids: Zondervan Publishing House, 1977).

[16] Gordon Allport, *The Individual and His Religion* (New York: Macmillan Co., 1960).

[17] Viktor Frankl, *Man's Search for Meaning* (New York: Washington Square Press, 1963).

[18] Rollo May, *Love and Will* (New York: W. W. Norton and Co., 1969).

[19] Eric Fromm, *The Revolution of Hope* (New York: Bantam Books, 1968).

[20] Abraham Maslow, *The Psychology of Science* (Chicago: Regnery Co., 1969).

[21] *Newsweek*, 21 June 1971, p. 66.

[22] B. F. Skinner, *Walden Two* (New York: Macmillan Co., 1962).

[23] Idem, *Beyond Freedom and Dignity* (New York: Knopf, 1971).

[24] Ibid., p. 18.

[25] Delgado, *Physical Control of the Mind*.

[26] B. Hoebel and P. Teitelbaum, "Hypothalamic Control of Feeding and Self Stimulation," *Science* 135 (1962): 375–377.

[27] Delgado, *Physical Control of the Mind*, pp. 170–71.

[28] Elliot Valenstein, *Brain Control* (New York: Wiley, 1973), p. 87.

[29] Delgado, *Physical Control of the Mind*, p. 168.

[30] Pribram, *Languages of the Brain*, p. 192.

[31] H. E. King, "Psychological Effects of Excitation in the Limbic System," pp. 477–486, in D. E. Sheer (ed.), *Electrical Stimulation of the Brain* (Austin: University of Texas Press, 1961), quoted in Delgado, *Physical Control of the Mind*, p. 139.

[32] P. E. McGhee and V. C. Crandall, "Beliefs in Internal-External Control of Reinforcements and Academic Performance," *Child Development* 39 (1968): 91–102.

[33]C. Hayes, *The Ape in Our House* (New York: Harper and Row, 1951).

[34]R. A. Gardner and B. T. Gardner, "Teaching Sign Language to a Chimpanzee," *Science* 165 (1969): 664–672. D. Premack, "The Education of Sarah: A Chimp Learns the Language," *Psychology Today* 4 (1970): 54–58. D. Premack, "Language in Chimpanzee?" *Science* 172 (1971): 808–822.

[35]Helen Keller, *The Story of My Life* (Garden City, N.Y.: Doubleday, Page and Co., 1902), quoted in Frank Severin (ed.), *Discovering Man in Psychology: A Humanistic Approach* (New York: McGraw-Hill Book Co., 1973), pp. 142–43.

[36]Ronald W. Langacker, *Language and Its Structure* (New York: Harcourt, Brace and World, 1967).

[37]Noam Chomsky, "A Review of *Verbal Behavior* by B. F. Skinner," *Language* 35 (1959): 26–58.

[38]Arthur C. Custance, *Man in Adam and in Christ* (Grand Rapids: Zondervan Publishing House, 1975), pp. 64–65.

[39]"Shanidar: The Cave with Soul," *Science News* 108 (1975): 343.

[40]Edwin A. Locke, "Determinism," *American Psychologist* 19 (1964): 846–847.

[41]Gunther Stent, "Limits to the Scientific Understanding of Man," *Science* 187 (1975): 1057.

[42]C. S. Lewis, *The Abolition of Man* (New York: Macmillan Co., 1947), p. 84.

[43]Genesis 1:26,27.

[44]Psalm 8:4,5, King James Version.

For Further Reading

Journal of the American Scientific Affiliation. Published by American Scientific Affiliation. Suite 450, 5 Douglas Avenue, Elgin, Ill., 60120.

This journal is published by a large affiliation of Christian scholars. Its articles deal primarily with science, psychology, and evolution.

Jeeves, Malcolm. **Psychology & Christianity: The View Both Ways.** Downers Grove, Ill.: InterVarsity Press, 1976.

This is an excellent book integrating psychology and Christianity by a professor of experimental neuropsychology.

MacKay, Donald. **The Clockwork Image.** Downers Grove, Ill.: InterVarsity Press, 1974.

MacKay, a specialist in brain physiology, has written a Christian perspective on science and determinism in this book.

Meehl, Paul, et. al. (ed.). **What, Then, Is Man? A Symposium of Theology, Psychology, and Psychiatry.** St. Louis, Mo.: Concordia Publishing House, 1958.

This is one of the most scholarly sources available for examining the issues on the nature of man and mental health from a Christian perspective.

Schaeffer, Francis. **Back to Freedom and Dignity.** Downers Grove, Ill.: InterVarsity Press, 1972.

This is a short book in which Francis Schaeffer deals with some current science that seeks to dehumanize man. There is excellent discussion of the ramifications of accepting chemical evolution and psychological determinism.

Smith, A. E. Wilder. **Man's Origin, Man's Destiny.** Wheaton, Ill.: Harold Shaw Publishers, 1968.

The author, who is holder of three Ph.D.'s in the sciences, discusses the scientific problems with evolution.

Notes